Better Business Writing

Become a more powerful communicator

Fifth Edition

Susan L. Brock

Viva Books
New Delhi | Mumbai | Chennai | Kolkata
Bengaluru | Hyderabad | Kochi | Guwahati

First Indian Edition 2011

VIVA BOOKS PRIVATE LIMITED

- 4737/23 Ansari Road, Daryaganj, New Delhi 110 002
  E-mail: vivadelhi@vivagroupindia.net, Tel. 42242200
- 76, Service Industries, Shirvane, Sector 1, Nerul, Navi Mumbai 400 706
  E-mail: vivamumbai@vivagroupindia.net, Tel. 27721273, 27721274
- Jamals Fazal Chambers, 26 Greams Road, Chennai 600 006
  E-mail: vivachennai@vivagroupindia.net, Tel. 28290304, 28294241
- B-103, Jindal Towers, 21/1A/3 Darga Road, Kolkata 700 017
  E-mail: vivakolkata@vivagroupindia.net, Tel. 22836381, 22816713
- 7, Sovereign Park Apartments, 56-58, K. R. Road, Basavanagudi, Bengaluru 560 004
  E-mail: vivabangalore@vivagroupindia.net, Tel. 26607409, 26607410
- 101-102 Mughal Marc Aptt., 3-4-637 to 641, Narayanguda, Hyderabad 500 029
  E-mail: vivahyderabad@vivagroupindia.net, Tel. 27564481, 27564482
- First Floor, Beevi Towers, SRM Road, Kaloor, Kochi 682 018, Kerala
  E-mail: vivakochi@vivagroupindia.net, Tel: 0484-2403055, 2403056
- 232, GNB Road, Beside UCO Bank, Silpukhuri, Guwahati 781 003
  E-mail: vivaguwahati@vivagroupindia.net, Tel: 0361-2666386

www.vivagroupindia.com

Published by arrangement with

Axzo Press, LLC
562, Willow Brook Office Park
Fairport, New York 14450

ISBN : 978-81-309-1832-7

Published by Vinod Vasishtha for Viva Books Private Limited, 4737/23, Ansari Road, Daryaganj, New Delhi - 110 002. Printed and bound by Raj Press, R-3, Inderpuri, New Delhi - 110 012.

Table of Contents

About the Author

Sue Brock (M.A. Communication) has taught full-time for the Communication Studies department at Cal Poly, San Luís Obispo, since 2002. She has also taught business communication in Cal State Hayward's Department of Marketing and in the Communication Studies Department at San José State University.

Before coming to Cal Poly, Sue worked for 15 years in communication consulting for Coopers & Lybrand, Barclays Global Investors, and Merrill Lynch in San Francisco; and for Financial Engines, Inc., an Internet startup company in Palo Alto. Her consulting work includes investment education, benefits consulting, and speech writing, and she continues to work with a variety of groups, including office assistants, engineers, and executives.

She is the author of *Writing Business Proposals and Reports* and the coauthor of *Writing a Human Resource Manual*.

Preface

American businesses reportedly lose more than $1 billion a year because of "foggy" writing that wastes time, kills contracts, and alienates customers. You don't have to be part of this problem. This book is designed to teach you the basics you need to become a better writer. The accompanying exercises will enhance your writing skills and are relevant to the practical demands of the business world. By the time you complete this brief book, you'll be better prepared to write a clear, concise business letter, memo, email, and report.

The best way to improve your writing is to write often. You'll find that, if you routinely practice the techniques in this book, your writing skills will continue to improve. When this happens, you'll be on your way to writing more clearly, concisely, and humanely, and this will make you more effective at work.

A voluntary learning contract is available in the Appendix. It's a good starting point, if you're serious about getting the most from this book. Good luck and don't give up! Writing well is hard work, but increasing your chances for a more successful career is worth it.

Susan Brock

Susan Brock

How Well Do You Know Your Writing Abilities?

Take a minute to assess your writing style. You may discover that you know a lot more than you think, or you may discover specific areas where you need to improve. Either way, this exercise will help you assess your writing ability. Read each statement and mark the response that applies to you.

	Yes	No	Don't Know
1. I consider my reader's perspective when I write.	❑	❑	❑
2. I have no problems with the basics: grammar, spelling, and punctuation.	❑	❑	❑
3. I know the difference between active and passive voice.	❑	❑	❑
4. I try to choose simple words to communicate clearly.	❑	❑	❑
5. I clearly state the purpose of my letters, memos, and emails.	❑	❑	❑
6. I recognize and avoid business clichés and jargon.	❑	❑	❑
7. I ruthlessly edit everything I write.	❑	❑	❑
8. I prefer simple words to communicate clearly.	❑	❑	❑

Don't worry if you weren't sure of the significance of any of these items. As you proceed through this book, you'll read explanations of each. Soon you'll be able to check Yes for each statement in this self-assessment!

Learning Objectives

Complete this book, and you'll know how to:

1) Review the basics of spelling, punctuation, and usage
2) Understand practical principles for sharpening your writing style
3) Explore ways to improve business memos, emails, and letters
4) Learn about writing bad news and writing to persuade
5) Understand personality types to improve business communication

Workplace and Management Competencies mapping

For over 30 years, business and industry has utilized competency models to select employees. The trend to use competency-based approaches in education and training, assessment, and development of workers has experienced a more recent emergence within the Employment and Training Administration (ETA), a division of the United States Department of Labor.

The ETA's General Competency Model Framework spans a wide array of competencies from the more basic competencies, such as reading and writing, to more advanced occupation-specific competencies. The Viva-Crisp Series finds its home in what the ETA refers to as the Workplace Competencies and the Management Competencies.

Better Business Writing covers information vital to mastering the following competencies:

Workplace Competencies:

- Customer Focus
- Checking, Examining, & Recording

Management Competencies:

- Informing

About the Viva-Crisp 50-Minute Series

The Viva-Crisp 50-Minute Series is designed to cover critical business and professional development topics in the shortest possible time. Our easy-to-read, easy-to-understand format can be used for self-study or for classroom training. With a wealth of hands-on exercises, the 50-Minute books keep you engaged and help you retain critical skills.

What You Need to Know

We designed the Viva-Crisp 50-Minute Series to be as self-explanatory as possible. But there are a few things you should know before you begin the book.

Exercises

Exercises look like this:

EXERCISE TITLE

Questions and other information would be here.

Keep a pencil handy. Any time you see an exercise, you should try to complete it. If the exercise has specific answers, an answer key is provided in the appendix. (Some exercises ask you to think about your own opinions or situation; these types of exercises don't have answer keys.)

Forms

A heading like this means that the rest of the page is a form:

FORMHEAD

Forms are meant to be reusable. You might want to make a photocopy of a form before you fill it out, so that you can use it again later.

A Note to Instructors

We've tried to make the Viva-Crisp 50-Minute Series books as useful as possible as classroom training manuals. Here are some of the features we provide for instructors:

- PowerPoint presentations
- Answer keys
- Assessments
- Customization

PowerPoint Presentations

You can download a PowerPoint presentation for this book from our Web site at www.CrispSeries.com.

Answer keys

If an exercise has specific answers, an answer key will be provided in the appendix. (Some exercises ask you to think about your own opinions or situation; these types of exercises will not have answer keys.)

Assessments

For each 50-Minute Series book, we have developed a 35- to 50-item assessment. The assessment for this book is available at www.CrispSeries.com. *Assessments should not be used in any employee-selection process.*

PART 1

Back to the Basics

"All the fun is in how you say a thing."

–Robert Frost

In this part:

- Mastering Spelling, Punctuation, and Usage
- Six Tips for Better Spelling
- Punctuation Pointers

Mastering Spelling, Punctuation, and Usage

You may be approaching this section with discomfort. Have no fear. You'll find that it's relatively painless—in part because it's short—but also because it concentrates on the most common errors people make.

Many people acquire bad habits in mechanics and usage before leaving school. The purpose of this section is to strengthen your skills in spelling, punctuation, and word usage. If this section does nothing more than correct a single error you repeatedly make, your writing will improve because of it.

"And this is the wall I stared holes into when I was writing my last memo."

Six Tips for Better Spelling

How many times have you checked a word in a dictionary, only to refer to the dictionary again for the same word because you couldn't remember the correct spelling? Following are six tips to help you correctly spell some problem words.

1. Basic Method

Using your senses (seeing, saying, hearing, visualizing, writing) can aid your memory for how words are spelled.

- Use a dictionary.
- Look at the word in syllables.
- Say it aloud in syllables.
- Visualize it and say it aloud.
- Write it out fully.

2. Shortcuts Method

Sometimes all we need to remember how to spell our most troublesome words is to use a mnemonic (memory aid) device.

- Locate the trouble spot in a word (the place where you misspell it).
- Isolate the sound.
- Underline the trouble spot.
- Emphasize it by mispronouncing it with the correct letter sound: Sep—A—Rate; Fa—Ti—Gue.
- Look for short words in the long word:
    - Argument (gum)
    - Environment (iron)
    - Cemetery (met)

3. Gimmicks

You can make up your own gimmick to help you remember how to spell words that are troublesome for you. Here are a few ideas:

- Question: What would you yell in a cemetery? Answer: Eee! (Remember that *cemetery* has three *e*'s.)
- The accident occurred on the RR tracks. (Remember that *occurred* has two *r*'s.)
- Loose as a goose. (Use rhymes to remember that *loose* has two *o*'s.)
- A Rat In The House Might Eat The Ice Cream (Use acronyms: The first letter of each word spells *arithmetic*.)
- The capitol building has a dome. (Remember that when referring to the building, *capitol* is spelled with an *ol* rather than an *al*.)

4. Spelling Tricks

Remember this rhyme from elementary school?

> Use *i* before *e*
>
> Except after *c*
>
> And when sounded like *a*
>
> As in *neighbor* and *weigh*

This spelling rule applies to more than 1,000 words. Can you think of some exceptions to the rule? Here are a few: *neither*, *weird*, *sheik*, *either*, *seize*, *leisure*.

5. To Double or Not to Double?

Occurred or occured? Which is it? Do you have trouble remembering if words such as *occur* have one or two *r*'s before adding an ending, such as *ed*?

Here is a trick. Take a look at the following lists of words:

Accent on first syllable	Accent on second syllable
layered	occurred
offered	referring
traveled	preferred
canceled	remitting
benefited	omitted
layered	occurred
totaled	permitted

Do you see a pattern? Notice that the words in the first list don't double the last consonant before adding *ing* or *ed*, and the words in the second list *do* double the last consonant in these cases.

One reason *offered* doesn't double the *r* and *referred* does is that you pronounce *offer* with the accent (or stress) on the first syllable. Say it aloud (OFF' er). Now say *refer* aloud (re FER').

So here's the rule for doubling or not doubling the final consonant before adding an ending:

- If the accent is on the first syllable, don't double the final consonant.
- If the accent is on the second syllable, do double the final consonant.

Note that some words may be spelled either way. For example:

- canceled or cancelled
- traveled or travelled
- programed or programmed

If you're in doubt, check your dictionary. But if you use the doubling rule, you don't have to remember which words can be spelled either way. By following the rule, you'll be able to figure out when to double and when not to. This doubling rule applies to more than 3,000 words.

6. Endings: Is it •able or •ible

- Add *able* to a full word:
  - adapt → adaptable
  - work → workable
  - love → lovable
    (Drop the *e* before adding the ending.)
  - desire → desirable
    (Again, drop the second *e* before the ending.)
  - change → changeable
    (The *e* stays this time! That's because it's needed to keep the *g* sound soft—as in *fringe*—rather than hard—as in *log*.)
  - desire → desirable
    (Again, drop the second *e* before the ending.)
  - manage → manageable
    (Same rule applies to keep the *g* soft.)

- Add *ible* if the root word is not a word by itself.
  - credible
    (*Cred* is not a word when it stands by itself.)
  - tangible

- Add *ible* to words that end in *x*, *ns*, and *miss*.
  - flexible
  - responsible
  - permissible

About Spell Check

The spell-check feature of word processing software highlights words that aren't in the computer's dictionary. These could include misspelled words, proper names, such as Acme Corporation, and initials or acronyms, such as HMO, CPA, and NASA.

The good news is that spell check finds and corrects many words you've misspelled. But it doesn't find and correct those words you have misused without misspelling them, such as the following:

affect	instead of	effect
there	instead of	their or they're
to	instead of	too or two
where	instead of	wear
imply	instead of	infer
bear	instead of	bare
wry	instead of	rye
compliment	instead of	complement
comprise	instead of	compose
manger	instead of	manager

In short, spell check can be a useful tool, but it's no substitute for careful proofreading!

CHECK YOUR SPELLING

Fill in the missing letters to spell the word correctly.

1. Many companies want to hire people who are ______ (flex-ble)
2. Ms. Brown wanted us to sit ______ (tog-th-r) at the meeting so we wouldn't be ______ (sep-r-ted) when the meeting was over.
3. The new hotel can ______ (acco-date) up to 1,500 guests.
4. This memo ______ (super-edes) the ______ (prec-ding) one, which was distributed last week.
5. The hospital ______ (ben-fit) raised a lot of money for the children's wing.
6. It never ______ (oc-ur-ed) to us that the ______ (gove-ment) might increase our taxes.
7. Her manager ______ (of-er-ed) her a bonus if she would ______ (proc-d) to enroll in a computer class.
8. We avoided an ______ (arg-ment) when we discussed changing the office ______ (envi-ment) to boost employee morale.
9. That part of the machine is ______ (l-se), and we're afraid that, if it falls off, we might ______ (l-se) it.
10. It would be difficult not to ______ (bel-ve) the results.

Compare your answers with those of the author in the Appendix.

Punctuation Pointers

For spelling, individuals usually fall into one of two categories—good spellers or poor spellers. Punctuation errors, on the other hand, can trouble everyone.

Fortunately, of the 30 main punctuation marks, business writing requires fewer than a dozen. Of these, the comma, colon, semicolon, and apostrophe are used most often—and often incorrectly!

The next few pages touch on only the highlights of the punctuation pointers, but you should find solutions here to many of the problems that trouble you.

Comma (,)

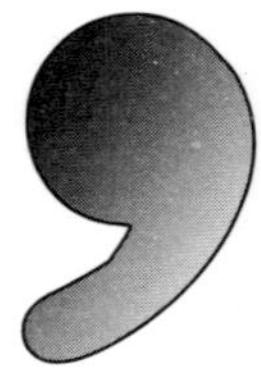

The comma sets off or separates words or groups of words within sentences.

Six Rules for the Comma

1. Use a comma after a long introductory phrase.
   After working all day at the office, I went home for dinner.

2. If the introductory phrase is short, forget the comma.
   After work I went home for dinner.

3. Use a comma if the sentence would be confusing without it.
   The day before, I borrowed her calculator.
   When you've finished, your dinner is ready.

4. Use a comma to separate items in a series.
   I need to pack my computer, calculator, business cards, and toothbrush.

5. Use a comma to separate two sentences that are joined by *and, but, or, nor, for, so, yet.*
   He wanted the promotion, but he was afraid to ask his manager.
   She liked her new job, and she respected her colleagues.
   They may go to the game, or they may stay here.
   The partners aren't going to the retreat, nor are they happy about it.
   Her assistant took a cab, for it was a long way to walk.
   They waited until Friday, so it was too late to go.
   I'd like to travel, yet I'm reluctant to change jobs.

6. Use a comma to set off nonessential elements in a sentence.

   At the podium stood a man wearing a green tie.

   At the podium stood Frank, wearing a green tie.

   In the first sentence, "wearing a green tie" is used to identify a specific man. Without it, the reader would not know to whom the writer was referring, so it's essential to the meaning of the sentence.

   In the second sentence, the writer assumes the reader knows Frank. "Wearing a green tie" adds only descriptive information about Frank, but it isn't essential to the meaning of the sentence.

Here's another example:

The computer that's in the hallway is brand new. (The writer identifies one particular computer "in the hallway," rather than the computer that's somewhere else. The location is essential to the sentence.)

The computer, which is in the hallway, is brand new. (The writer assumes there's only one computer and adds only descriptive information—"in the hallway"—that's nonessential to the meaning of the sentence.)

A Common Comma No-No

Do not separate two independent statements with a comma.

He bought his first car last fall, it never ran well.

You can correct this sentence in any of the following ways:

- Use a period in place of the comma

  He bought his first car last fall. It never ran well.

- Use a comma plus a conjunction (and, but, or, nor, so, for, yet)

  He bought his first car last fall, but it never ran well.

- Use a semicolon

  He bought his first car last fall; it never ran well.

Semicolon (;)

The semicolon separates two independent clauses in one sentence when you want to keep the two thoughts more tightly linked than if the clauses were two separate sentences: "I type letters; he types bills."

Use a semicolon before and a comma after the following words, if the words come between two independent clauses.

accordingly	hence	moreover	similarly
also	however	namely	still
besides	likewise	nevertheless	then
consequently	indeed	nonetheless	therefore
furthermore	instead	otherwise	thus

Examples:

> *I thought I'd completed the project; consequently, I was surprised to hear about the additional work.*
>
> *We have prepared your estimate; however, you shouldn't sign it before Friday.*
>
> *The partners' retreat will take place in March; therefore, all business matters will be discussed then.*

Colon (:)

A colon is a tipoff to get ready for what's next: a list, a long quotation, or an explanation. A colon can separate independent clauses when the second clause explains or amplifies the first.

> *My new office contains the following items: a desk lamp, a swivel chair, and an inbox that's always full.*
>
> *Fred was proud of his sister: She'd been promoted to managing partner.*
>
> *There are two things to remember in a job interview: Always arrive promptly and always dress appropriately.*

Note in the above examples that, if the statement following the colon is an independent clause, the first word of the statement is capitalized.

Apostrophe (’)

An apostrophe is used to form the *possessive* of nouns and some pronouns or to mark the omission of a letter or letters in a contraction. In the contraction *can’t*, for example, the apostrophe replaces the letters *no* from *cannot*. An apostrophe isno’ used to make a singular noun plural.

Here are some guidelines for forming possessives:

- If the noun is singular, add *’s*

  I enjoyed Betty’s presentation.

  Someone’s coat is in the lobby.

- The same applies for singular nouns ending in *s* such as Chris

  This is Chris’s new office.

- If the noun is plural, add an apostrophe after the *s*

  Those are the clients’ files.

- If the singular noun ends in *s* (such as Jones), add *es* and an apostrophe to make it both plural and possessive

  Here is the Joneses’ tax information.

ADD THE PUNCTUATION

Punctuate the sentences below. Not all of the sentences need additional punctuation.

1. The executive watched the competition but the competition went ahead with the takeover.
2. During our meeting she was genial but shrewd.
3. Today more women are becoming executives in corporations.
4. The job was difficult therefore he quit.
5. My briefcase contained files pencils books and paper.
6. We thought we would have to work late consequently we were happy to be home before dark.
7. My managers car was in the shop however she borrowed her husbands.
8. In preparation for the meeting Mr. Jones asked us to do three things set up the equipment clear the tables and close the blinds.
9. We wanted to go to the partners meeting but we were unable to leave before the weekend.
10. Alexis résumé arrived yesterday moreover he phoned for an interview next week.

Compare your answers with those of the author in the Appendix.

Spelling and Punctuation

Correct punctuation and spelling in the following letter.

March 29, 20XX

Mr. John C. Fremont
2929 East Sycamore Street
Chicago IL 60601

Dear Mr. Freemont:

Thank you for meeting with us, and for your time and effort in preparing for the intervue. We appreciate your accomodating us with a flexable schedule.

We are in the final stages of procesing your application and we need three more items for our files. Your social security number permanent home address and date of birth; as soon as we get this information we can procede to complete your permanent records.

Everyone here at Southwestern Corporation is looking forward to working with you. And we are eager to have you begin as soon as possible. Please, call me as soon as you can with this information.

Sincerely,

Janet L. Estes

Senor Vice President

/jle

Compare your answers with those of the author in the Appendix.

WORD USAGE QUIZ

Sometimes writers have trouble deciding the proper word to use—especially when words sound alike. Test your knowledge of proper word usage by circling the correct answer(s) for each item below.

1. The (**effect** or **affect**) of wearing seatbelts can (**effect** or **affect**) the number of people injured in automobile accidents.

2. Paine's *Common Sense* (**effected** or **affected**) a turnaround of public opinion, which had a dramatic (**effect** or **affect**) on the fight for liberty.

3. Which is correct, **a** or **b**?

   a. I promise not to raise taxes, which would be harmful to the economy.

   b. I promise not to raise taxes that would be harmful to the economy.

4. (**A** or **An**) historic choice?

5. He (**implied** or **inferred**) that we were not to blame.

6. This memo will (**supercede** or **supersede**) the one we wrote last week.

7. There (**seem** or **seems**) to be problems with the way management operates.

8. Neither my manager nor the partners (**goes** or **go**) to the meetings.

9. The comittee is (**comprised** or **composed**) of volunteers like yourselves.

10. Complete each sentence using either **capital** or **capitol.**

    Austin is the __________ of Texas.

    The company tried to raise enough __________ to buy new equipment.

    Paris is the __________ of France.

    The first word of every sentence should begin with a __________ letter.

    The senator met with the press on the steps of the __________ building.

Compare your answers with those of the author in the Appendix.

Proper word usage is covered well in *The Elements of Style*, by William Strunk and E.B. White, and *On Writing Well*, by William Zinsser.

Part Summary

In this part, you learned how to improve **spelling**, **usage**, and **punctuation**. You learned how to use **six tips** for better spelling. Then, you learned how to use the **comma**, **semicolon**, **colon**, and **apostrophe** properly. Finally, you learned some tips on **word usage**.

PART 2

Choosing Your Words Carefully

"The difference between the almost right word and the right word is really a large matter—it's the difference between the lightning bug and the lightning."

–Mark Twain

In this part:

- Sharpening Your Writing Style
- Deleting (Unnecessary) Redundancies
- Forming Parallel Construction
- Recognizing Clichés
- Avoiding Sexist Language

Sharpening Your Writing Style

In writing, *style* means how language is used. The meaning of your message often can be stated in endless ways with most readers understanding what you mean. But a writing style that is unclear, clumsy, or weak can bog down and distract the reader to the point that the message itself becomes obscured. On the other hand, learning and using good style makes writing easy to read and understand. Ideally, the reader doesn't even notice the style.

Listed below are 10 common pitfalls that can spoil your writing style and lessen clarity, crispness, and vigor in your correspondence. You may personalize this list by jotting down other pitfalls you've encountered.

1. Too many words
2. Too many big words
3. Jargon
4. Vague expressions
5. Condescending statements
6. Negative expressions
7. Inattention to detail
8. Inattention to the reader
9. Lack of commitment
10. Passive construction
11. ____

    ____

"I guess you missed the memo about Victorian Friday."

Too Many Words

> ***"The most valuable of all talents is that of never using two words when one will do."***
>
> **–Thomas Jefferson, Author, Declaration of Independence**

As Mr. Jefferson observed, one word is better than two. A good rule is to limit your sentences to fewer than 17 words each. Edit ruthlessly.

Not: In this letter we've attempted to answer all of your questions, and we hope that if you have any additional questions whatsoever, you will not hesitate to contact us.

But: If you have questions, please call.

Overuse of Big Words

> ***"I never write "metropolis" for seven cents, because I can get the same money for "city." I never write "policeman," because I can get the same price for "cop."***
>
> **–Mark Twain**

Keep your writing simple: Use *home* rather than *abode*, *face* rather than *visage*, *use* rather than *utilize.*

Short words are better than long words. Try to be natural in your writing. Read your letters aloud after you write them; they should sound human and conversational.

Not: Pursuant to our discussion, herewith we acknowledge receipt of your correspondence as of the above date.

But: We received your letter on December 16 as we discussed.

Trim the Fat

Can you simplify to improve the expressions on this list? This exercise helps identify and eliminate wordiness, which editors sometimes call *fat*. The first two are examples.

Expression	Simplified
terminate the illumination	turn the lights out
revenue commitment	tax increase
at this point in time	
in the event of	
due to the fact that	
at a later date	
on a daily basis	
each and every one	
firstly	
in my opinion, I think	
irregardless	
owing to the fact that	
there is no doubt but that	
clenched tightly	
close proximity	
in the majority of instances	
in an intelligent manner	

Compare your answers with those of the author in the Appendix.

For a good book on eliminating wordiness, read *Fat-Free Writing* by Carol Andrus, Axzo Press.

Jargon

Consider your reader. Avoid unexplained terms such as *facilitator* and *interface*. What's a *modified departmentalized schedule*? The more general the readership, the less jargon you should use. If jargon must be used and there's any question someone won't know its meaning, define the jargon term in parentheses the first time it appears.

Not: Our facilitator will interface with the new communication systems network.

But: Our administrative assistant will operate the new telephone system.

Vague Expressions

Be concise and specific. If the "profits were affected," did they increase or decrease?

Not: The company's negative cash flow position forced it to right-size its operations to the level of profitable market opportunities.

But: The company lost money and had to lay off workers.

Condescending Statements

Write with warmth, as one human to another. "Of course" can be interpreted as "as any idiot knows."

Not: We are certain you are concerned with saving money. Of course, you will mail the enclosed card. We thank you in advance.

But: If saving money is important to you, please mail the enclosed card today. Thank you.

Negative Expressions

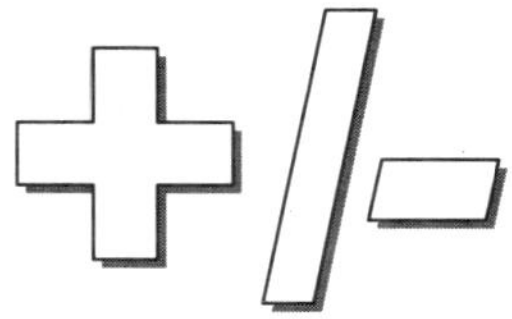

Stress the positive. Rather than telling what you can't do or don't have, provide good news.

Not: We're sorry to tell you that we don't carry XYZ software.

But: We're sending you a list of distributors who carry XYZ software because we no longer offer this product.

Inattention to Detail

Double-check accuracy and quality. Reread for typos and misspelled words. Obvious errors make readers suspicious of the credibility of the source, regardless of the subject matter.

Not: We hope we can accomodate your office supply and stationary needs.

But: We hope we can accommodate your office supply and stationery needs.

Inattention to the Reader

Write from the readers' perspective. What's in it for them? This means it may be more appropriate to write in the second person (you) than in the first person (I, we).

Not: We would like to invite you to attend the conference. (first person)

But: You're invited to attend the conference. (second person)

Not: Direct deposit will save money for our company. (first person)

But: You'll have immediate access to your money on payday thanks to the new direct deposit system our company has started. (second person)

Lack of Commitment

Take a stand. Omit qualifiers such as *sort of*, *rather*, *quite*, *somewhat*, which serve only to weaken your statement.

Not: We're quite pleased about our rather exciting word processor.

But: We're pleased about our exciting line of word processors.

Passive Construction

Use active verbs. The standard order of sentences is *subject* (performer of action), *verb* (action), and *object* (receiver of action). In passive construction, the order is reversed: The object is first, followed by a form of the verb ***be*** (*am*, *is*, *are*, *was*, *were*, *have been*, *is being*) with the main verb. The subject is last, usually preceded by the word *by*.

Passive: The check was signed by my supervisor. (7 words)

The letter is being typed by the assistant. (8 words)

He practices what has been taught. (By whom is implied.)

Active: My supervisor signed the check. (5 words)

The assistant is typing the letter. (6 words)

He practices what the trainer taught us.

Sometimes the subject of the sentence is omitted from passive constructions.

Passive: An employee's extra efforts should be recognized. (by whom?)

Active: Managers should recognize an employee's extra efforts.

Passive: Enclosed are your schedules.

Active: I am enclosing your schedules.

Active construction is almost always more direct, more economical, and more forceful than passive construction

As you proofread your work, consider making your writing more active by using the verb forms of *be* cautiously. Their overuse weakens your writing.

Passive Voice—An Active Writing Exercise

Revise these sentences so that all main verbs are in the active voice. Leave the space blank if the sentence is already in the active voice. For example:

Passive: The consultant was hired by the manager.

Active: The manager hired the consultant.

1. Our request for an increase in salary will be considered by the board at its next meeting.

2. Our inability to agree is seen by management as a weakness.

3. The decision on the annual budget is always made by our board of directors.

4. Incorrect data on the computer should be deleted.

5. Our office manager will speak to us on Monday.

CONTINUED

CONTINUED

6. It will be necessary to downsize the organization's marketing department.

7. Problems should be reported to the office manager.

8. The check was signed by my supervisor.

9. Please be advised that these adjustments should be completed immediately.

10. The jobs were completed by the management team.

Compare your answers with those of the author in the Appendix.

Deleting (Unnecessary) Redundancies

Sometimes writers use too many words because of redundant expressions. And the more words that readers have to wade through to get to the point of the correspondence, the more likely you are to lose their attention.

Look closely at the list below. Many of these expressions sound right because we hear them so often, but you can delete the word or words in parentheses with no loss in meaning. Notice how many words are unnecessary.

(advance) planning
ask (a question)
(as to) whether
(as) yet
(at a) later (date)
at (the) present (time)
(basic) fundamentals
(specific) example
(but) nevertheless
(close) proximity
(close) scrutiny
combine (together)
(completely) filled
consensus (of opinion)
continue (on)
estimated at (about)
(exact) opposites
first (of all)
for (a period of) 10 days
(just) exactly
my (personal) opinion
(absolutely) essential

(as) for example
refer (back)
(true) facts
(when and) if
whether (or not)
written (down)
(brief) moment
off (of)
period (of time)
might (possibly)
since (the time when)
recur (again)
(still) remains
(thorough) investigation
sufficient (enough)
started (off) with
merged (together)
repeat (again)
blend (together)
came (at a time) when
(false) pretenses
(on a) daily (basis)

Word Weeds

Now that you've learned to recognize and eliminate wordiness, this exercise provides additional practice pruning what you write. Rewrite each without losing the original meaning.

1. It has been my wish for a considerable period of time to gain entrance into the field of accounting. This is due to the fact that challenges of my intellect are what challenge me.

2. To me it appears that Smith did not give any attention whatsoever to the suggestion that had been recommended by the consultant.

3. In the past there were quite a large number of firms located on the West Coast offering us competition. At this present point in time, the majority of those firms have been forced to go out of business by the hardships and difficulties of the present recessionary period of business contraction and stagnation.

4. It is the policy of this company in every case to proceed with care in testing each and every new product under development by us, and such testing must precede our arriving at any positive conclusion with respect to the effectiveness of said product.

5. In the event that Wilkins does not come forth with an expression of willingness to lend us assistance in the matter of financing this project, it is entirely conceivable that we will not be able to make the required acquisitions of raw materials we need without help.

Compare your answers with those of the author in the Appendix.

Forming Parallel Construction

Parallel construction adds clarity, elegance, and symmetry to your writing. Words, phrases, and statements are coordinated to be grammatically parallel: noun aligned with noun, verb with verb, and phrase with phrase.

Not: Speaking in public is sometimes harder than to write in private.

But: Speaking in public is sometimes harder than writing in private.

Not: My partner is a man of action, decisive, and who is bright.

But: My partner is a man of action, decision, and intelligence.

Not: Sarah's office was painted, had carpeting put in, and paneled last week.

But: Sarah's office was painted, carpeted, and paneled last week.

Not: To teach, to supervise, and delegating work are a few of the tasks our office manager performs.

But: To teach, to supervise, and to delegate work are a few of the tasks our office manager performs.

Or: Teaching, supervising, and delegating work are a few of the tasks our office manager performs.

Not only does parallel construction add symmetry, it often reduces wordiness, as you can see in some of the examples above. Don't hesitate, however, to repeat a word if it makes your sentence clearer. For example:

Not: She has and continues to seem competent.

But: She has seemed and continues to seem competent.

Not: You can program the computer to check the grammar but not think.

But: You can program the computer to check the grammar but not to think.

When you proofread your work, check for parallel construction. The added clarity and economy will add polish to your style.

Make It Parallel

Revise the following sentences to form correct parallel construction. If the sentence is already parallel, leave the space blank.

1. It was both a long meeting and very tedious.

2. Joe likes a job with challenging work that keeps him stimulated.

3. Poor writing wastes time, costs money, and customers feel alienated.

4. This would eliminate continual errors, repeated corrections, unnecessary memos, and, most important, the time spent on each.

5. His experience made him sullen, bitter, and a cynic.

6. Our instructor drilled us, tested us, and he also gave us encouragement.

7. I went to Maui to enjoy the warm weather and for getting some practice in snorkeling.

CONTINUED

CONTINUED

8. I plunged into the water, swam away from shore, and made my first dive.

____

____

9. Our first choice is John, who is healthy, witty, capable, and an athlete.

____

____

10. The personnel officer told me that the clerk would answer the phone, greet the visitors, distribute mail, and some typing.

____

____

11. On a resume: Hobbies: swimming, reading, bicycling, and piano

____

____

12. On a multi-media slide during a business presentation:

What We Can Do For You:

Increase your cash flow

Improve your customer relationships

Reduce employee turnover

New business development

____

____

____

____

13. Sometimes, going to meetings is as exciting as watching paint dry.

____

____

Compare your answers with the author's solutions in the back of the book.

Recognizing Clichés

A cliché is any trite or fad word or phrase that has become overused or commonplace, such as *input*, *parameters*, *utilize*, *hopefully*, and *enclosed please find*. The problem with clichés is that they rob your writing of force and originality, boring your reader in the process.

Not: Enclosed please find the information per your request. Hopefully, you can utilize our product to benefit your company within the parameters of your computer's invoice processing. We appreciate your input.

But: We've enclosed the information you requested. Our product will speed your computer's invoice processing. Thank you for your suggestions.

Learn to recognize and avoid trite expressions and clichés such as these:

along these lines
as per our agreement
at the present time
due to the fact that
enclosed please find
for the purpose of
in response to your memo of
in view of the fact
per
pursuant to
regarding the matter of
we are returning herewith
as per your request
at an early date
despite the fact that
enclosed herewith
for the amount of
in response to your letter of
pending receipt of
please be advised
thank you for your cooperation
we will file your letter for future reference
with reference to your letter of
subsequent to

Avoiding Sexist Language

The increasing number of women in business has changed many traditional practices, including the use of language. The English language has, for centuries, used the masculine singular pronoun *he* when the person to whom the pronoun is referring could be either male or female.

For example, "The average American worker changes jobs eight times in *his* career" was the correct form in traditional grammar. Nowadays, such grammar rules are evolving to avoid sexism and to make the language gender-neutral.

As Karen Judd points out in *Copyediting, Third Edition: A Practical Guide*, it isn't always possible to correct sexist language, but some things can be done. Here are a few hints:

1. Recast sentences into the plural to avoid gender references.

   Not: An accountant must pass a difficult exam before he can become a CPA.

   But: Accountants must pass a difficult exam before they can become CPAs.

2. Reword sentences to eliminate unnecessary gender references.

   Not: An accountant must pass a difficult exam before he can become a CPA.

   But: An accountant must pass a difficult exam before becoming a CPA.

   Or: An accountant must pass a difficult exam to become a CPA.

3. Use the second person form when appropriate (if you know your audience):

   Not: An accountant must pass a difficult exam before he can become a CPA.

   But: As an accountant, you must pass a difficult exam before you can become a CPA.

4. Use the construction *he or she* sparingly, where rewriting sentences in one of the above ways would be awkward. Or alternate references throughout a report or manuscript, sometimes using *he,* sometimes *she*.

5. Don't characterize professions by sex:

   Not: Girl Friday; stewardess; male nurse; lady lawyer

   But: Administrative assistant; flight attendant; nurse; lawyer

6. Avoid, wherever practical, words that use the suffix *-man* in the traditional sense of *male*. Pay attention to common, current usage. This doesn't mean inventing words, but just being sensitive to women's participation in all areas.

   Not: Chairman; foreman; spokesman; fireman; policeman

   But: Chair or chairperson; supervisor; spokesperson (*or* spokeswoman); fire fighter; police officer

7. Use nonsexist and more specific forms of address in salutations of business correspondence.

   Not: Gentlemen; Dear Sirs

   But: Dear Partners; Dear Members; Dear Doctors; and the like

Many companies omit the salutation and complimentary close. Letters are simplified to emphasize their message and streamline their form. The following letter demonstrates this idea.

A Business Letter

March 26, 20XX

Human Resources Manager
Sanders Enterprises, Inc.
1425 Seaview Way
Daly City, CA 93456

Special Phone System[1]

We have established a special phone system to improve the communication between employment counselors and employers. Please call our office any afternoon between 4 and 5 P.M. if you have questions about available applicants or if you would just like to talk. We believe that, if we encourage employers to call, we can establish a closer relationship with you and better meet your staffing needs.

Ted F. Jones

Employment Counselor

---

[1] This subject line may be centered as it is or placed flush left to conform with the letter's block style.

Part Summary

In this part, you learned how to **choose** your words carefully. You learned how to avoid **too many** words. You also learned to avoid **big words** and **jargon**. Next, you learned the pitfalls of **vague** expressions, **condescending** statements, and **negative** expressions. You learned how to focus attention on **detail** and on the **reader**. Then, you learned how to address lack of **commitment** and to rewrite **passive** construction. You learned how to eliminate **redundancies** and how to form **parallel** constructions. Finally, you learned how to avoid **clichés** and **sexist language**.

P A R T **3**

Improving Your Business Writing

"I try to leave out the parts that people skip."

–Elmore Leonard

In this part:

- Strengthening Your Memos
- Using Email Effectively
- Ten Tips for a Better Memo
- How to Begin

Strengthening Your Memos

This part contains writing samples of memos that exemplify weaknesses and errors common in business writing. Some of the weaknesses are subtler than others. Please read each sample carefully and evaluate each stage: the *before* version, the *corrected* version, and the *improved* version.

Note how much more direct and clear the revised versions are. The sentences are brief and to the point, and the improved versions sound natural and conversational without being too informal.

"Leo, I love the roar you put into your quarterly report."

Accountant's Memo

John Freeman, president of ABC Enterprises, asked his accountant to explain why his accounting bill doubled since last year. His accountant writes a memo to respond.

Before version:

Dear John:

In response to your letter of June 15, 20XX, enclosed please find Exhibit A. As you can see, the work performed for you this year is different than last year. In addition, the parameters of tasks increased since last year. Accordingly due to this fact and the fact that our billing rates were raised this year; it was necessary to increase our charges for professional services rendered. Hopefully, this letter offers some explanation as to the question you raised. If you require more additional information, please don't hesitate to contact us.

Corrected version:

Dear John:

In response to your letter [trite] of June 15, 20XX, [condescending] enclosed please find [cliché] Exhibit A. As you can see, [condescending] the work performed for you this year is different than [use "from"] last year. In addition, the parameters [jargon] of tasks increased since last year. Accordingly due to this fact [omit] and the fact that our billing rates were raised this year; it was necessary [passive] to increase our charges for professional services rendered. Hopefully, [omit] this letter offers some explanation [use "answers"] as to the question you raised. If you require more additional [redundant] information, please don't hesitate to contact us. [wordy]

Improved version:

Dear John:

We understand your concern, and we hope the following will answer your questions about the increase in your bill.

1. Last year we spent 12 hours (@ $200/hour) preparing two tax returns for you.
2. This year we spent 15 hours (@ $250/hour) preparing four tax returns for you.
3. This year we successfully represented you in an audit with the Internal Revenue Service (3 hours @ 250/hour).
4. This year we produced monthly financial statements for you, but last year we produced quarterly financial statements.

Please call me if you would like to discuss this further. We value you as a client.

The Employment Counselor's Memo

An employment agency counselor is announcing his company's new telephone communication setup to current and prospective clients.

Before version:

Dear Employer:

We have established a special phone communication system to provide additional opportunities for your input. During this year we will give added emphasis to the goal of communication and utilize a variety of means to accomplish this goal. Your input, from the unique position of employer, will help us to plan and implement an effective plan that meets the staffing needs of your company. An open dialogue, feedback and sharing of information between employment counselors and employers will enable us to work with your staffing needs in the most effective manner.

Corrected version:

Dear Employer:

We have established a special phone communication system [vague] to provide additional opportunities for your input. [jargon] During this year we will give added emphasis to the goal of communication and utilize [use "use"] a variety of means to accomplish this goal. Your input, [jargon] from the unique position [unclear] of employer, will help us to plan and implement an effective plan that meets the staffing needs of your company. An open dialogue, feedback and sharing of information [stilted] between employment counselors and employers will enable us to work with your staffing needs in the most effective manner. [wordy]

Improved version:

Dear Employer:

We have established a special phone system to improve the communication between employment counselors and employers. Please call our office any afternoon between 4 and 5 P.M. if you have questions about available applicants or if you would just like to talk. We believe that if we encourage you to call, we can establish a closer relationship and better meet your staffing needs.

The Sales Manager's Memo

A sales manager asked her administrative assistant to send a memo (with a copy of quarterly sales figures) to the sales staff, asking them to meet with her on the following Friday. The assistant writes the following memo.

Before version:

To: All Sales Representatives

From: Julie Martin

Date: July 15 (year)

Subj: Sales Meeting

RE phone contact of July 8, final sales totals for the quarter ended June are enclosed herewith. A planning conference for all sales personnel will be scheduled for the near future and these figures will be discussed. It is hoped that all district managers will be aware that the figures are such that reductions in the total number of dealerships and retail units may be indicated. A meeting to discuss this matter will be held on Friday, 18 July, at 3 P.M., in the regional manager's office. Thank you for your cooperation.

Improved version:

To: All Sales Representatives

From: Julie Martin

Date: July 15 (year)

Subj: Sales Meeting

Please join me for a sales meeting on Friday, July 18, at 3 P.M. in the regional manager's office. We will discuss the attached quarterly sales totals.

This meeting is important, because we may have to reduce dealerships and retail units.

Using Email Effectively

Email has made communicating with others quicker than ever. Long gone are the days when secretaries typed their bosses' letters to send to customers or clients. Today, most managers type letters for themselves.

The good news is that administrative assistants are able to take on more challenging work for a more satisfying career, and everyone is able to respond faster to colleagues, clients, and customers. The bad news is that email's informality has led people to cut etiquette corners in their email messages.

Remember, no matter how you communicate with them, clients and customers still deserve respect and consideration. And, equally important, your written communications are a reflection of you and your professionalism. Just as in other business writing, always use proper spelling, punctuation, and sentence structure; and proofread your emails before sending them. If you're most efficient when you brainstorm and organize on paper first, then do that before writing the email. It could save you from sending a hastily prepared message.

Following are guidelines for making the most of email technology in business. The "Ten Tips for a Better Memo" later in this section apply to email messages as well.

Pay Attention to Tone

Because email is less formal than a letter but more formal than a conversation, it's important that your email "sounds" professional and pleasant even if your words are strong. And never use all capitals—IT COMES ACROSS AS SHOUTING.

Reread your email aloud before you send it to make sure you don't sound snide, insulting, or sarcastic— even inadvertently. If you're writing an email when you're angry, follow the sage advice of waiting until the next day to reread it. Then send it only if it sounds professional.

Along the same line, don't be too flip and cute with the overuse of email jargon or emoticons like ;-). Even though they can communicate quickly, make sure your readers are receptive to such informalities before you use them.

Write Informative Subject Lines

We often screen our emails by scanning subject lines. Readers may discard (without reading) messages that don't seem relevant or clear. To get your emails read, use specific subject lines, such as "Request to reschedule meeting" or "How Project XYZ will save $500K per year." These subject lines communicate your message, even if the recipient doesn't read the entire email.

When you reply to an email, change the subject line, if necessary, to communicate more directly. Reply to "Request to reschedule meeting" with "Meeting rescheduled to May 31," or respond to "How Project XYZ will save $500K per year" with "Okay, I'm sold: Let's do Project XYZ."

Consider Format

Email messages are most effective if kept short. But if you must send a lengthy message, forecast the structure. On your readers' first screen, summarize your message and then indicate what's to come with a listing of your section headings. You can ease reading long passages by using the same devices you see in the newspaper:

- Headings
- White space
- Occasional all caps, bolds, and underling
- Indents
- Lists

What you see on your screen may not be what your reader sees. If your readers' computer systems are different from yours, your line lengths can cause an annoying text-wrap effect on their screens. To be safe, keep your lines to 55 or 60 characters, including spaces. Exaggerate any indentation you use to make sure it "catches" on your readers' screens.

Send Attachments with Care

Because of virus concerns, many people routinely delete emails with unsolicited attachments, especially if they're in a compressed format. So make sure the attachments you send are wanted. When in doubt, ask first.

Size matters, too. Some attachments are huge files that take up a lot of space and can take significant time to download. Use appropriate file formats and compression programs when warranted, or use file transfer protocols such as ftp.

Reply to the Right People

As easy as it is to hit "Reply All" and send your email to everyone on the list, no one likes to receive unnecessary mail. It falls into the "spamming" camp in some people's minds. Make sure your emails are meaningful for the people who receive them.

Treat Email like an Open Book

Anyone who receives your message can easily forward it verbatim to others, including those you may never have intended to see it. Thus, a good rule of thumb is to pretend your email is a postcard—open to everyone—even if marked confidential.

Don't Count on Immediacy

Email is a convenient way to send and receive messages, but it isn't always read immediately. If you expect a prompt response, use the telephone. For example, if you're sending an email to invite people to a meeting that's an hour away, don't expect much of a turnout.

Some email systems have a feature that notifies you when someone has received and read your email. If that service is important to you, spend some time learning how to implement it and other useful features of your system.

Even if your recipients don't respond as quickly as you'd like, you can do your senders a service by replying promptly to their messages. Don't negate one of the main advantages of email—speed.

Keep these points in mind, and you'll have fewer regrets about emails you send.

For more information on the effective use of email for business communications, read *Writing Effective Email*, by Nancy Flynn and Tom Flynn, Axzo Press.

Ten Tips for a Better Memo

No matter what your position in your organization, good written communication skills make every other part of your job easier. Follow these 10 tips for each memo and email message you write.

1. Get to the point quickly—the reader already knows the purpose of the memo from the subject line. Make sure your subject line is clear and to the point.
2. Be interesting, conversational, and natural.
3. Highlight key ideas (*,-, or •); make it readable.
4. Keep it short—generally use 17 or fewer words per sentence.
5. Write in A-B-C order (sequentially).
6. If your message includes several questions requiring a response, number them. This makes it easier for the recipient to respond.
7. Be specific, clear, concise, and economical.
8. Keep your reader(s) in mind.
9. Keep it simple.
10. Keep it to one page.

Memo Editing

This is a memo from the president of XYZ Company to all employees. Revise this memo on a separate sheet of paper to make it clearer, shorter, and friendlier.

To: All Employees

From: The President

Date: September 15, 20XX

Re: Staff Meeting Postponement

XYZ Company wishes to inform all employees of the postponement of the previously scheduled staff meeting. This cancellation is due to the fact of a current pressing financial situation in this company.

This firm has faced a significant drop in sales volume for the past six months. Our response to these pressing issues must be to make more productive use of our time and effect an increase in the sales volume.

This staff meeting will be postponed immediately until further notice by the president. Employees will be informed of further developments regarding rescheduling our meeting and our financial situation.

Compare your revision to the author's in the Appendix.

How to Begin

Sometimes, no matter how long you stare at the blinking cursor on your otherwise blank computer screen, you can't figure out how to begin. When this happens to you, a good starting point is to:

1. Write these words:

   "I want to tell you that…"

2. Tell what you want to tell.
3. Delete the six words at the beginning and see what you have left.

These steps at least get you started, so you have a rough draft to revise and polish.

Here is an example:

1. Dear Dr. Ames:

   I want to tell you that…

2. Dear Dr. Ames:

   I want to tell you that we need to reschedule your tax appointment for an earlier time on Friday.

3. Dear Dr. Ames:

   We need to reschedule your tax appointment for an earlier time on Friday.

Now this writer can continue the letter to provide additional information, such as the reason for the change, a suggested alternative appointment time, and so on.

LETTER EDITING

Even if you spend a lot of time writing for business, you may find yourself spending even more time editing. As you move up through the managerial ranks, you're likely to edit letters, memos, and reports written by others.

The following exercise offers some practice in editing letters. Read through the three paragraphs below; then edit directly on the letter to make it clearer, more concise, and more grammatically correct. You may rewrite sentences, but make sure that the original meaning is not lost.

March 16, 20XX

Annette Clark
Marketing Director
Central Coast Boat Fabrics
1493 Main Street
Morro Bay, CA 93442

Dear Annette:

Thank you for bringing to are attention your product. Kevlar is a good material to make boat hulls out of because it is not heavy like other hull fabrics and since it is used to make bulletproof vests and tank armor it is strong. It is difficult to punctuate a boat made of kevlar.

Unfortunately, kevlar is expensive and kevlar is very difficult to work with due to it's strength. We at the present time do not have the necessary tools to work with this fabric.

For now, we will continue to construct the boats that we make out of fiberglass. As soon as we are ready for kevlar, however, you can be sure that your company will be carefully considered as a kevlar supplier.

Sincerely,

A.J. Smith

Compare your edits with those of the author in the Appendix.

Part Summary

In this part, you learned how to **strengthen** your memos by working with before-and-after versions of memos. Next, you learned how to use **email** effectively. You learned **ten tips** you can use to write better memos. Finally, you learned steps for **beginning** a memo.

PART 4

Writing for Special Circumstances

"People with tact have less to retract."

–**Arnold H. Glasow**

In this part:

- Special Kinds of Business Writing
- Conveying Bad News Tactfully
- When the News Is Especially Sensitive
- Writing Persuasively
- Using the Motivated Sequence Online

Special Kinds of Business Writing

Congratulations on your progress! Now that you've practiced the basics, you're ready to move forward. In this section, you'll have the opportunity to learn how to write for two kinds of situations: when you must convey bad news and when you want to persuade.

Writing Bad News

Often in business we must break bad news to good people. Whether you're rejecting an applicant for a job, turning down an employee's request for a raise, or breaking the news to a customer that you're out of widgets, writing bad news isn't fun—but it's often necessary. And doing it well can help you keep good business relationships.

This section addresses strategies and techniques for conveying bad news tactfully, clearly, and kindly.

Writing to Persuade

Another kind of business communication that requires special handling is persuasive writing. A lot of business writing is persuasive. Cover letters that accompany resumes are designed to sell the applicant, sales letters are designed to sell the product, proposals are designed to sell services, and reports are often designed to sell recommendations or solutions to problems.

This section will show you how to develop your writing to make it more persuasive.

Conveying Bad News Tactfully

Most business writing emphasizes brevity in the interest of respecting your reader's time. But when conveying bad news, brevity takes a back seat to tact and tone. Choose your words carefully, selecting words that are courteous and positive.

Don't use qualifiers, passive construction, or euphemisms to avoid accepting responsibility.

For example, a company president wrote the following to her employees:

> *It is necessary to resize our operation to the level of profitable market opportunities.*

What she meant was this:

> *We must lay off staff.*

A memo to correct an employee's behavior is more effective if sentences begin with a word other than "you," as you can see in the negative and positive example phrases below. Whenever possible, avoid overusing the finger-pointing "you" in favor of a more positive tone.

Negative	**Positive**
You failed to notice...	*May I point out that...*
You neglected to mention...	*We also can consider...*
You overlooked the fact...	*One additional fact is...*
You missed the point...	*From another perspective...*
If you persist in...	*If you choose to...*
I see no alternative but...	*Our clear plan of action...*

How to Say No

At times, an employee's request must be denied. Be direct and considerate, but don't be too subtle or you may mislead by offering false hope rather than communicating clearly. Remember, even criticism can be delivered positively.

The sample memos below address an employee who has been eagerly awaiting a transfer to the organization's San Francisco office. The HR manager has been asked to write a memo to tell him the transfer won't take place.

Note the difference in packaging between the "before" and "improved" memos. Both versions deny the request, but the "before" sounds mechanical, stuffy, and cold. Although you want to be clear and concise in your writing, don't sacrifice kindness. When you must give bad news, take the time to select words that are tactful and kind.

Before:

> To: John Williams
> From: Marsha Brown
> Date: May 12, 20XX
>
> Re: Denial of your request for transfer
>
> I regret to inform you that your request for transfer to our San Francisco office has been denied. At this point in time, there are no positions open for which you are qualified. Thank you for your understanding.

Improved:

> To: John Williams
> From: Marsha Brown
> Date: May 12, 20XX
>
> Re: Response to transfer request
>
> After we spoke last week, I checked into the possibility of your transferring to our San Francisco office. Unfortunately, I learned that a transfer isn't possible for two reasons. First, our department needs your experience and skills for new product marketing. Second, this year San Francisco is expanding only its accounting department.
>
> I'm sorry your proposed transfer won't work out. Please let me know if I can assist you in any other way.

Some managers might avoid the second version because it provides material for the employee to debate the decision: "But Dave can take over my work here!" or "I heard through the grapevine that San Francisco is expanding its marketing department, too." Good managers realize that, if the employees have these concerns, then these conversations need to take place. Writing in a way that tries to preempt them may seems safe and time-saving, but it's neither good writing nor good management.

Break the Bad News

Let's say you manage an employee who seems to lack motivation. The employee arrives late to work, dresses inappropriately, and doesn't finish assigned tasks. In the space below or on a separate sheet of paper, write a memo to motivate the employee. Supply additional information as needed.

Compare your efforts with those of the author in the Appendix.

THE BAD NEWS BUSINESS LETTER

You should now be prepared to write a complete letter using the information you have learned. Mark Smith has applied for a position with your firm for which he won't be hired. As you write the rejection letter, keep in mind that he has good qualifications and that you'd like more information about him should another position come open.

Refer to the preceding sections as you organize your thoughts, and remember to avoid the common pitfalls of business writing. Use the space below to begin your outline, then draft your letter on a separate sheet. Although your letter will be different from the model, it will be well written if you avoid unnecessary words, jargon, or vague words.

Compare your efforts with those of the author in the Appendix.

When the News Is Especially Sensitive

It can be difficult to convey the bad news of turning down an applicant, rejecting an employee's request, or notifying customers of inventory shortages. Such communications are relatively routine, however, compared to delivering especially sensitive news, such as an employee's life-threatening illness or death or the company's response to a serious workplace accident. But the same guidelines apply no matter how sensitive the bad news:

- Be tactful.
- Keep the tone positive and courteous.
- Avoid qualifiers, passive construction, and euphemisms.
- Be direct and considerate without being too subtle.
- Express appropriate concern.

Example: Communicating Concern

A manager in a large organization was given the following assignment after a key assistant in the public relations department had been on sick leave for several weeks. The assistant was diagnosed with HIV and asked the manager to write a memo to all staff, with full disclosure of the illness, to prepare them for the assistant's return to work on the following Monday.

As you read the memo, note how clear, kind, and concerned the manager sounds for both his assistant and for the other employees.

> Date: February 15, 20XX
>
> As most of you know, David McDermott has been a key member of our public relations staff for nearly three years. In his new role as assistant manager, he continues to provide the timely, quality support that we have all come to depend on since his arrival in our group. Now it's our turn to show him just how supportive we can be.
>
> I know that you share my feelings of concern for David, and I hope you'll help him in any way possible when he returns. If you have questions or concerns, please contact me or Anna Chin in Human Resources.

Writing Persuasively

Some people avoid using the word *persuasion*, because it conjures images of manipulation and deceit. This is unfortunate because most communication is persuasive. Any time you influence or affect people, you're being persuasive. And everything you write in business—memos, emails, invoices, or client proposal letters—affects the reader.

This section provides information on communicating persuasively and offers you an opportunity to write a persuasive letter using skills you've acquired in this book.

Here's a good first rule: Show how your reader will benefit. Don't tell clients and prospects how great your photocopier is—tell them how great their copies will look.

As Aristotle said, "The fool tells me his reasons, but the wise man persuades me with my own."

"Your boss called. He asked me not to let you watch any television until you finish writing your opening statement."

An excellent self-study book on persuasive writing is *Writing Persuasively*, by Kathleen A. Begley, Axzo Press.

Using the Motivated Sequence Outline

When you're preparing a persuasive letter, report, or speech, the Motivated Sequence Outline is an effective tool for organizing your points. To be effective, persuasive letters must include the following five steps:

1. Get readers' attention.
2. Show readers how a problem affects them.
3. Solve the problem.
4. Explain what your solution will do.
5. Encourage readers to adopt your solution.

The Motivated Sequence Outline on the next page takes you step by step through each of these requirements. But before you begin working through the outline, write a complete sentence stating exactly what you hope to accomplish in the letter you'll write. This will give you focus. Remember this purpose to keep your message on track as you outline your letter.

1. Attention Step
   - Overcome readers' apathy.
   - Use illustration, example, etc.
2. Need Step
   - Show why change is needed.
   - Show why readers need to feel affected by the problem.
3. Satisfaction (of Need) Step
   - State solution.
   - Demonstrate that solution is logical, sensible, and feasible.
   - Convince that solution will solve problem.
   - Give examples where solution has worked.
4. Visualization (of Future) Step
   - Show readers what solution will do for them.
   - State advantages.
5. Action Step
   - Convince readers to adopt solution.
   - Tell readers what you want them to do.
   - Direct readers to act.

Drafting a Letter with the Motivated Sequence Outline

The following letter exemplifies how the Motivated Sequence Outline was used to draft a letter to attract customers to Elite Travel Agency for vacation planning.

Elite Travel Agency
333 California Street
San Francisco, CA 94111

April 19, 20XX

Ms. Kathleen Atwood
204 London Street
Oakland, CA 94605

Dear Ms. Atwood:

(Attention) If you don't like romance, beautiful places, and friendly people, stop reading now.

(Need) But if you need to get away from the pressures of work... if you'd enjoy the exhilaration of bicycling through green pastures and rustic villages... if you want to be welcomed with open arms by people known for their warm hospitality... then a guided bicycle tour through Ireland, one of Europe's most breathtaking countries, is for you.

(Satisfaction) Elite Travel is offering discount prices for folks like you who wish to spend a splendid summer vacation experiencing a new culture in a foreign land—at a price so low you can't afford to pass it up. Prices for 10-day tours begin at only $3,979, including airfare, bike rentals, three meals a day, and lodging.

(Visualization) Imagine bicycling on well-maintained trails, stopping at points of historical interest and incredible views, including castles, battlegrounds, and lands where old Irish tales come to life. Each day we'll stop, tired and happy, at favorite bed and breakfast inns for delicious meals, hot baths, and luxuriating sleep.

(Action) If this package sounds good, call us today. Join us for a vacation you'll talk about for years. Call toll free at 1-800-555-0900 before this offer ends on April 30. Don't miss out! We're going to have a great summer, and we'd love to have you along.

Sincerely,

Dan Edwards
Manager

ATTRACT YOUR READER'S ATTENTION

A well-written *attention* paragraph is crucial to encourage your reader to read through to the last paragraph, often called the *action* paragraph. Many people, however, find it difficult to write the opening paragraph to any letter—particularly if the letter is persuasive. But once you successfully develop your opening ideas, your remaining thoughts usually flow more naturally.

In the space below, practice writing an attention-getting opening paragraph to introduce the gourmet café you're opening on a university campus. The café serves breakfast and lunch. Remember, your goal in the first paragraph—the attention paragraph—is to arouse the interest of both students and faculty. Try to select strategies that will appeal to both audiences.

After you finish writing your paragraph, read on to see alternative ways of developing an opener designed to grab the attention of your audiences.

Sample 1

Are you tired of eating the same old greasy hamburgers and fries? Or tasteless vending-machine food? Does eating on campus remind you of eating on an airplane? Does "campus food" sound like an oxymoron? Prepare for a change!

Sample 2

Imagine walking to class and experiencing the aroma of freshly baked breads and hearty, flavorful soups. Picture yourself sitting at a cozy table enjoying a rare roast beef sandwich, or spinach and lentil soup with a fresh sourdough baguette, or grilled swordfish with fennel, capers, and sun-dried tomatoes.

Scrutinizing the Samples

Note how each of the sample openers includes specifics to appeal to students and faculty. Typically, students are on budgets, so mentioning reasonable prices would be a sound strategy to appeal to students who have little money. And if it's true that a wider variety of food, including more exotic fare, would appeal to an older, more sophisticated crowd (such as university faculty), then describing tantalizing foods might pique their interest.

Note, too, the style of each opener. Sample 1 uses a sentence fragment, an incomplete sentence—"Or tasteless vending-machine food?"—to make a point. In professional writing, complete sentences are more appropriate than fragments. But in a sales letter designed to capture attention, formal writing rules tend to bend a bit.

The second sample includes descriptions that appeal to the senses—"freshly baked," "rare roast beef." Arousing your readers' senses so they can almost see, hear, taste, or smell can be a good attention-getting strategy.

Part Summary

In this part, you learned how to write for special situations such as **persuading** or delivering **bad news**. You learned how to take extra measures when bad news is **especially sensitive**. Finally, you learned how to use a **Motivated Sequence Outline** when writing to persuade.

PART 5

Know Your Audience

"Those who write clearly have readers. Those who write obscurely have commentators."

–Albert Camus

In this part:

- Identifying Communication Styles
- Writing to Specific Styles
- Ten Techniques for Effective Communication
- Voluntary Learning Contract

Identifying Communication Styles

Before you begin to write, you must consider your audience. If you have some insight into the personality of your reader, you'll have the opportunity to tailor your writing to make it compatible with that personality. What could be more flattering to readers than to receive a letter or memo written with them in mind? The addition of a human element is so often missing in the business world.

Tailoring your writing to specific personality types begins with identifying the four general communication styles, based on Swiss Psychologist Carl Jung's theory. These styles are:

- Sensor/Action Style
- Thinker/Process Style
- Feeler/People Style
- Intuitor/Idea Style

Identifying a person's communication style isn't a method for figuring them out. Most people exhibit traits from each of the styles from time to time. Still, one communication style is generally dominant. And it's to this style that you should tailor your business writing. Let's look at each style in more detail.

Sensor/Action Style

People who are strong in this style like action: doing, achieving, getting things done, improving, and solving problems.

Description: action-oriented, results-oriented, task-oriented, workaholic, confident, hard-charging, determined, tough, competitive.

Strengths: pragmatic, assertive, directive, competitive, confident, disciplined in using time, receptive to options.

Weaknesses: domineering, arrogant, status-seeking, emotionally cold, impulsive, autocratic, inattentive, impersonal.

Common jobs: athlete, manager, executive, coach, truck driver, entrepreneur, pilot, doctor.

Opposite style: Intuitor/Idea.

Both styles (Sensor/Action and Intuitor/Idea) convey how people gather information. People with Sensor/Action style gather information by using their senses (hearing, seeing, etc.); those with Intuitor/Idea style gather information by using their intuition or by listening to their gut feelings.

Thinker/Process Style

People who are process-oriented like fact-finding, organizing, and setting up strategies and tactics.

Description: analytical, logical, self-controlled, stubborn, detail-oriented, aloof, critical, skeptical, conservative, noncommittal.

Strengths: perfectionist, well-organized, objective, rational, conceptual, persistent, accurate, orderly, hard working.

Weaknesses: indecisive, insensitive, inflexible, slow, judgmental.

Common jobs: accountant, banker, attorney, doctor, scientist, clerk, engineer, computer programmer, teacher.

Opposite style: Feeler/People.

Thinking/Process styles andFeeler/People styles are opposites, because they convey how people make decisions. People with Thinking/Process style make decisions based on facts and data; those with Feeler/People style make decisions based on what's best for the group.

Sensor/Action and Thinker/Process styles are both common in the business world. The two styles use different approaches to letters. The Thinker/Process style emphasizes thoroughness and detail; the Sensor/Action style seeks to know the bottom line. Consider the communication style of your reader in everything you write.

Feeler/People Style

Individuals who are people-oriented like to focus on social processes, interactions, communication, teamwork, social systems, and motivation.

Description: emotional, caring, introspective, melancholic, sympathetic, diplomatic, persuasive, entertaining, warm, friendly, agreeable, dependable, stable.

Strengths: spontaneous, persuasive, empathic, probing, loyal, warm, supportive, dependable, sensitive.

Weaknesses: impulsive, sentimental, procrastinating, subjective, overly sensitive, overly cautious.

Common jobs: nurse, administrator, teacher, social worker, sales associate, psychiatrist, trainer.

Opposite style: Thinker/Process

Intuitor/Idea Style

People with the idea orientation like concepts, theories, idea exchanges, innovation, creativity, and novelty.

Description: creative, reflective, quiet, scholarly, reserved, conceptual, intelligent, enthusiastic, personable, gregarious, impatient, involved, assertive.

Strengths: original, conceptual, warm, approachable, stimulating, adventurous, sensitive, receptive to new ideas, creative, idealistic, flexible.

Weaknesses: unrealistic, devious, impractical, manipulative, undisciplined in use of time, uncontrolled.

Common jobs: scientist, researcher, artist, professor, writer, corporate planner, advertising person, stockbroker.

Opposite style: Sensor/Action

Feeler/People and Intuitor/Idea styles are becoming more common in the business world. Your letters to readers possessing these traits need to be human. Because so much business writing seems mechanical and computer-generated, those with the People and Idea styles will appreciate your remembering that writing is a personal transaction between people.

Sometimes she tested her business writing on a mixed audience.

Writing to Specific Styles

In the following examples, the sales letter from Part 4 has been adapted to address each style of reader.

Adapting to the Sensor/Action Style

Emphasize action, doing, achieving, getting things done, improving, and solving problems. Get to the point quickly. Don't waste their time. Be clear and specific.

Elite Travel Agency
333 California Street
San Francisco, CA 94111

April 19, 20XX

Ms. Kathleen Atwood
204 London Street
Oakland, CA 94605

Dear Ms. Atwood:

Get away from the pressures of work. Recharge your batteries. Do it today. Right now.

— Bike through Ireland.

— Stop at castles and battlegrounds.

— Work up an appetite for excellent meals.

— Revel in hot baths and down comforters.

— Gear up for the next day's trek.

Elite travel is offering busy people who like action and luxury—people like you—a travel package that costs so little you won't be able to pass it up.

You can join us for a 10-day tour, including airfare, bike rental, three meals per day, and lodging for only $3,979.

If this package sounds good, call us today. 1-800-555-0900. This offer expires on April 30. Don't miss out.

You've worked hard. You've earned it.

Sincerely,

Dan Edwards

Approaching the Thinker/Process Style

Emphasize facts, organizing, and structure. Provide more detail than for other styles. Appeal to logic and reason.

> Elite Travel Agency
> 333 California Street
> San Francisco, CA 94111
>
> April 19, 20XX
>
> Ms. Kathleen Atwood
> 204 London Street
> Oakland, CA 94605
>
> Dear Ms. Atwood:
>
> If saving money and getting away to a place that will recharge your batteries doesn't appeal to you, stop reading now.
>
> On the other hand, if you need to get away from the pressures of work and school and you'd enjoy the exhilaration and education of bicycling through the historical wonders of the Irish countryside, then a guided bike tour through Ireland may be just for you.
>
> If bicycling sounds too rigorous for a relaxing, restorative vacation, you have the option of signing up for the accompanying bus trip—your choice.
>
> Elite Travel is offering discount prices for people like you—people who would like to vacation in Ireland and experience a new culture at a price so low you can't afford to pass it up. Prices for 10-day tours are $3,979, including airfare, bike rental or bus fare, three meals per day, and lodging.
>
> You can find all the details about this package in the enclosed brochure. But remember: This offer expires on May 15.
>
> If this sounds good, call us toll free at 1-800-555-0900. We'll be glad to answer all your questions. Don't miss out. Join us for the vacation of a lifetime!
>
> Sincerely,
>
> Dan Edwards

Approaching the Feeler/People Style

Emphasize social processes, interactions, communication, and teamwork.

Elite Travel Agency
333 California Street
San Francisco, CA 94111

April 19, 20XX

Ms. Kathleen Atwood
204 London Street
Oakland, CA 94605

Dear Ms. Atwood:

If you don't like romance, beautiful places, and friendly people, stop reading now.

On the other hand, if you need to get away from the pressures of work, and you'd enjoy the exhilaration of bicycling with other enthusiastic travelers through green pastures and rustic villages, if you want to be welcomed with open arms by people known for their warm hospitality, then a guided bicycle tour through Ireland, one of Europe's friendliest and most breathtaking countries, is for you.

Elite Travel is offering discount prices for people like you—people who'd like to experience a new culture at unbeatably low prices. Prices for 10-day tours are $3,979, including airfare, bike rental, three meals a day, and lodging.

Throughout this tour we'll bicycle on well-maintained trails, stopping at historical points of interest with incredible views that include castles, battlegrounds, and villages where old Irish tales come to life. Each day we'll stop, tired and happy, at favorite bed and breakfast inns for delicious meals in a family atmosphere, hot baths, and luxuriating sleep.

If this sounds good, call us toll free today at 1-800-555-0900 before this offer expires on April 30. Join us for a vacation that you'll talk about for years. Don't miss out! We're going to have a terrific vacation, and we'd love to have you along.

Sincerely,

Dan Edwards

Enticing the Intuitor/Idea Style

Emphasize theories, exchange of ideas, innovation, creativity, and novelty.

Elite Travel Agency
333 California Street
San Francisco, CA 94111

April 19, 20XX

Ms. Kathleen Atwood
204 London Street
Oakland, CA 94605

Dear Ms. Atwood:

If you don't like romance, beautiful places, and friendly people, stop reading now.

On the other hand, if you'd enjoy the exhilaration of bicycling through green pastures and rustic villages, if you want to be welcomed with open arms by people known for their warm hospitality, then a guided tour through Ireland, one of Europe's friendliest and most breathtaking countries, is for you.

Imagine...

bicycling on well maintained trails,
stopping at historical battlegrounds,
enjoying incredible views of castles,
visiting villages where old Irish tales come to life.

Each day we'll stop, tired and happy, at favorite bed and breakfast inns for delicious meals, hot baths, and luxuriating sleep.

Elite Travel is offering discount prices for people like you—people who'd like to experience the adventure of a lifetime. Prices for 10-day tours are $3,979, including airfare, bike rental, three meals per day, and lodging.

If this sounds good, call us toll free today at 1-800-555-0900 before this offer expires on April 30. Join us for a vacation that you'll talk about for years. Don't miss out! We're going to have a terrific vacation, and we'd love to have you along.

Sincerely,

Dan Edwards

Ten Techniques for Effective Communication

Working toward better business writing leads in many directions. At first, you may find that old habits are hard to slip out of. You also may find that, when you try to improve your writing, it takes you longer to write even routine letters. You still may be tempted to use jargon and clichés. You may become frustrated as you stare at a blank computer screen or fill your wastebasket with crumpled paper. Don't despair! Writing is hard work, but the quality of the final product is the key to greater rewards.

The following list is a summary of the most important points discussed in this book. Make it a habit to read through the list to incorporate these techniques whenever you practice writing.

1. Keep your writing clear, concise, and simple.
2. Choose your words carefully.
3. Be natural.
4. Avoid fad words, jargon, and clichés.
5. Use active verbs; avoid passive construction.
6. Take a stand, make a commitment, avoid qualifiers.
7. Use familiar words—plain English.
8. Be specific: Avoid vagueness.
9. Eliminate redundant expressions.
10. Keep your audience in mind.

A useful companion book is *Writing Business Proposals and Reports*, by Susan Brock, Axzo Press.

Voluntary Learning Contract

We all have good intentions. What separates those who are successful from those who aren't is how well these good intentions are carried out.

A voluntary contract, or agreement, can help convert your good intentions into action.

The Voluntary Learning Contract is a good starting point if you're serious about getting the most from this book.

You or your supervisor can initiate this agreement either before you begin working in this book or after you've completed it.

VOLUNTARY LEARNING CONTRACT

I, ____,
(Print your name)

Agree to meet with the individual designated below, at the times shown, to discuss my writing skills progress. The purpose of all sessions will be to review my writing skills and establish action steps in areas where improvement still may be required.

I agree to meet with the above individual on:

____

____

____

____
(Describe schedule, giving dates and times)

____
(Signature of supervisor or instructor)

Areas needing attention:

- ❑ Spelling
- ❑ Punctuation
- ❑ Usage
- ❑ Style
- ❑ Writing Persuasively
- ❑ Other

____
(Your Signature) (Date)

Part Summary

In this part you learned how to identify four communication styles: **Sensor/Action**, **Thinker/Process**, **Feeler/People**, and **Intuitor/Idea**. You learned how to recognize the strengths, weaknesses, and opposites of each style. Next, you learned how to adapt and write to a **specific** style. Then, you learned how to use **ten techniques** for effective communication. Finally, you learned how to use a **voluntary learning contract** to reinforce the things that you learned from this book.

APPENDIX

Appendix to Part 1

Comments & Suggested Responses

Check Your Spelling

1. Many companies want to hire people who are flexible (flex-ble).
2. Ms. Brown wanted us to sit together (tog-th-r) at the meeting so we wouldn't be separated (sep-r-ted) when the meeting was over.
3. The new hotel can accommodate (acco-date) up to 1,500 guests.
4. This memo supersedes (super-edes) the preceding (prec-ding) one, which was distributed last week.
5. The hospital benefit (ben-fit) raised a lot of money for the children's wing.
6. It never occurred (oc-ur-ed) to us that the government (gove-ment) might increase our taxes.
7. The assistant's manager offered (of-er-ed) her a bonus if she'd proceed (proc-d) to enroll in a computer class.
8. We avoided an argument (arg-ment) when we discussed changing the office environment (envi-ment) to boost employee morale.
9. That part of the machine is loose, and we're afraid that if it falls off we might lose it.
10. It would be difficult not to believe (bel-ve) the results.

Add the Punctuation

1. The executive watched the competition, but the competition went ahead with the takeover.

2. During our meeting she was genial but shrewd.

   No punctuation needed. The introductory phrase is short and doesn't require a comma. Note there's no comma before the phrase "but shrewd" because it isn't an independent clause.

3. Today more women are becoming executives in corporations.

   No punctuation needed.

4. The job was difficult; therefore, he quit.

   Or: The job was difficult. Therefore, he quit.

   Or: The job was difficult, and therefore he quit.

   Or: The job was difficult, so he quit.

5. My briefcase contained files, pencils, books, and paper.

   Note: There's no colon after "contained," because a colon must follow a complete sentence such as the following:

   My briefcase contained four items: files, pencils, books, and paper.

6. We thought we would have to work late. Consequently, we were happy to be home before dark.

7. My manager's car was in the shop; however, she borrowed her husband's.

8. In preparation for the meeting, Mr. Jones asked us to do three things: set up the equipment, clear the tables, and close the blinds.

9. We wanted to go to the partners' meeting, but we were unable to leave before the weekend.

10. Alexis's résumé arrived yesterday; moreover, he phoned for an interview next week.

Spelling and Punctuation

Punctuation corrections are circled; spelling errors are lined out and corrected.

March 29, 20XX

Mr. John C. Fremont
2929 East Sycamore Street
Chicago, IL 60601

Dear Mr. ~~Freemont~~ Fremont:

Thank you for meeting with us, and for your time and effort in preparing for the ~~intervue~~ interview. We appreciate your ~~accomodating~~ accommodating us with a ~~flexable~~ flexible schedule.

We are in the final stages of ~~procesing~~ processing your application, and we need three more items for our files: your social security number, permanent home address, and your date of birth. As soon as we get this information, we can ~~procede~~ proceed to complete your permanent records.

Everyone here at Southwestern Corporation is looking forward to working with you, and we are eager to have you begin as soon as possible. Please, call me as soon as you can with this information.

Sincerely,

Janet L. Estes
~~Senor~~ Senior Vice President

/jle

Word Usage Quiz

Which is correct?

1. The **effect** [result] of wearing seatbelts can **affect** [influence] the number of people injured in automobile accidents.

   Effect can be used as noun or a verb. As a noun, it means result or outcome. As a verb, it means to bring about.

   Affect is usually used as a verb in business writing, and it means to influence.

2. Paine's Common Sense **effected** [brought about] a turnaround of public opinion, which had a dramatic **effect** [outcome] on the fight for liberty.

3. Which is correct, a or b?

   a. I promise not to raise taxes, which would be harmful to the economy.

   b. I promise not to raise taxes that would be harmful to the economy.

   The correct answer depends on the meaning. The first choice (a) is correct if the candidate promises not to raise any taxes (because raising any taxes would be harmful to the economy). The comma sets off nonessential elements in the sentence (see "Punctuation Pointers"), which means that the clause that follows the comma isn't essential to the meaning of the sentence.

   Second choice (b) says that the candidate won't raise any taxes harmful to the economy (implying that, if elected, the candidate could raise only those taxes that aren't harmful to the economy). To a voter, the difference between (a) and (b) could be important.

4. A historic choice.

5. Which is correct? That depends on the meaning.

   a. He implied that we weren't to blame. (Implied means suggested. Speakers imply.)

   b. He inferred that we weren't to blame. (Inferred means concluded. Listeners infer.)

6. This memo will **supersede** the one we wrote last week.

7. There **seem** to be problems with the way management operates.

   Problems is plural; therefore, seem is correct.

8. Neither my manager nor the partners **go** to the meetings.

   Although generally a singular verb follows neither and either, if one of the subjects is plural and one is singular, make the verb agree with the subject nearer to it. Partners is plural and is nearer to the verb.

9. The committee is composed of volunteers like yourself.

   If you really have a fondness for the word comprise, you could say:

   The committee comprises volunteers like yourself

   One way to keep these words straight is to remember that "comprise" means "include." You wouldn't say, "The committee is included of volunteers like yourselves."

10. Complete each sentence using either capital or capitol.

    Austin is the capital of Texas.

    The company tried to raise enough capital to buy new equipment.

    Paris is the capital of France.

    The first word of every sentence should begin with a capital letter.

    The senator met with the press on the steps of the capitol building.

    Use *capitol* only when referring to the building itself.

Appendix to Part 2

Comments & Suggested Responses

Trim the Fat

terminate the illumination	lights out
revenue commitment	tax increase
at this point in time	now
in the event of	if
due to the fact that	due to or because
at a later date	later
on a daily basis	daily
each and every one	all
firstly	first
in my opinion, I think	use one or the other (or none—opinion is implied)
irregardless	regardless
owing to the fact that	due to or because (of)
there is no doubt but that	undoubtedly or doubtless
clenched tightly	clenched
close proximity	close
in the majority of instances	usually
in an intelligent manner	intelligently

Passive Voice—An Active Writing Exercise

1. At their next meeting, the board will consider our increase in salary.
2. Management sees our inability to agree as a weakness.
3. Our board of directors makes the decision on the annual budget.
4. We should delete incorrect data on the computer.
5. [OK as is. Needs no revision.]
6. We need to lay off part of the organization's marketing department.
7. Report problems to the office manager.
8. My supervisor signed the check.
9. Please complete these adjustments immediately.
10. The management team completed the jobs.

Word Weeds

1. I have always wanted to go into accounting, because it challenges me.
2. I believe Smith ignored the consultant's suggestion.
3. Many of our West Coast competitors have gone out of business because of the recession.
4. It's company policy to test all new products carefully for effectiveness.
5. If Wilkins doesn't help us financially, we may not be able to acquire needed raw materials.

Make It Parallel

1. It was both a long and very tedious meeting.

2. Joe likes a job with challenging and stimulating work.
   Or: Joe likes a job that challenges him and that keeps him stimulated.

3. Poor writing wastes time, costs money, and alienates customers.

4. This would eliminate continual errors, repeated corrections, unnecessary memos, and, most important, wasted time.

5. His experience made him sullen, bitter, and cynical.

6. Our instructor drilled us, tested us, and encouraged us.

7. I went to Maui to enjoy the warm weather and to practice snorkeling.

8. I plunged into the water, swam away from shore, and made my first dive.

   [No change needed]

9. Our first choice is John, who is healthy, witty, capable, and athletic.

10. The personnel officer told me that the clerk would answer the phone, greet visitors, distribute mail, and type.

11. On a resume:

    Hobbies: swimming, reading, bicycling, and playing the piano

12. On an overhead transparency during a business presentation:

    What We Can Do For You:

    Increase your cash flow

    Improve your customer relationships

    Reduce employee turnover

    Develop new business

13. Sometimes, going to meetings is as exciting as watching paint dry.
    [No change needed]

Appendix to Part 3

Comments & Suggested Responses

Memo Editing

To: All Employees

From: The President

Date: September 15, 20XX

Re: Staff Meeting Postponement

To help get our sales volume back on track, we're postponing our staff meeting until early winter. We will let you know our meeting's new date as soon as we select it.

I appreciate your extra efforts and encourage you to be productive and work to increase sales during the 4th quarter.

This revision is just one approach to improving the memo. Here, the president uses a more personal tone (*We* rather than *XYZ Company* and *You* rather than *employees*). Using active (rather than passive) voice helps keep the information simpler, clearer, and shorter.

Letter Editing

Draft

March 16, 20XX

Annette Clark
Marketing Director
Central Coast Boat Fabrics
1493 Main Street
Morro Bay, CA 93442

Dear Annette:

Thank you for bringing to are attention your product. Kevlar is a good material to make boat hulls out of because it is not heavy like other hull fabrics and since it is used to make bulletproof vests and tank armor it is strong. It is difficult to punctuate a boat made of kevlar.

Unfortunately, kevlar is expensive and kevlar is very difficult to work with due to it's strength. We at the present time do not have the necessary tools to work with this fabric.

For now, we will continue to construct the boats that we make out of fiberglass. As soon as we are ready for kevlar, however, you can be sure that your company will be carefully considered as a kevlar supplier.

Sincerely,

A.J. Smith

Final

March 16, 20XX

Annette Clark

Marketing Director

Central Coast Boat Fabrics

1493 Main Street

Morro Bay, CA 93442

Dear Annette:

Thank you for bringing your product to our attention. Kevlar is a good material for boat hulls because it is strong, lightweight, and difficult to puncture. Unfortunately, Kevlar is also expensive and difficult to work with because of its strength. We do not have the necessary tools to work with this fabric.

For now, we will continue to construct our boats out of fiberglass, but as soon as we are ready for Kevlar, we will consider your company as a supplier.

Sincerely,

A.J. Smith

Appendix to Part 4

Comments & Suggested Responses

Break the Bad News

To: John Smith

From: Maria Jimenez

Date: September 1, 20XX

Re: Performance Update

As I look back over your work during the past six months, I'm convinced you can succeed in our marketing department. Recently, however, some of your work habits haven't been up to your usual high standards. Specifically, I'm referring to punctuality, appropriate dress, and timely task completion.

Punctuality: Arriving to work on time (8 A.M.) is extremely important to client service—especially when our clients are accustomed to calling us early, knowing their account manager will be here.

Appropriate Dress: Professional dress (as described in our Employee Handbook) from Monday through Thursday (with casual dress on Friday) is important, especially for those unexpected business presentations and client meetings.

Timely Task Completion: Deadlines are a constant here, so our general rule is, if you know you won't be able to complete a task on time, inform your supervisor immediately so that we'll have the time to reassign the task.

John, please see me if you have any questions; otherwise, I'm confident you'll get back on track this week. Let's meet on October 15 to follow up on these and other topics.

Author's note: Notice how Maria describes the positive behaviors she wants to see—rather than the more negative "inappropriate dress," "tardiness," and "not completing tasks."

The Bad News Business Letter

Mark Smith
100 Elm Street
Glenville, WA 98888

Dear Mark:

Thank you for applying to XYZ Corporation for the position of staff accountant. Although we do not have any openings now, we expect to interview again in December. Your resume is impressive, and we will keep it on file if a staff accountant position should become available before then.

Meanwhile, please send us three letters of recommendation to complete your application package. We appreciate your interest.

Sincerely,

XYZ Corporation

William R. Houghton

Viva-Crisp 50-Minute
Titles in the Series

ISBN	Author	Title	YOP	Price
9788130918174	Gambino	**50 Minutes to Better Software Demos**: *Apply Your Sales Skills with Confidence*	2011	195.00
9788130918488	Bozek	**50 One-Minute Tips to Better Communications**: *Speak, Write and Present More Effectively, 3/e*	2011	250.00
9788130918211	Conlow & Watsabaugh	**Achieving Supervisory Excellence**: *Be the Leader Your People Need*	2011	195.00
9788130918396	McKnight & Chapman	**Attitude**: *Protect Your Most Priceless Asset, 5/e*	2011	245.00
9788130918495	Terry Dickey	**Basics of Budgeting**: *Become a Better Business Planner, 2/e*	2011	250.00
9788130918310	Conlow & Watsabaugh	**Become a Successful Supervisor**: *Develop Essential People Skills*	2011	225.00
9788130918327	Brock	**Better Business Writing**: *Become A More Powerful Communicator, 5/e*	2011	225.00
9788130918228	Dupont	**Business Etiquette & Professionalism**: *Conduct Yourself With Confidence, 3/e*	2011	195.00
9788130918181	Morgan	**Calming Upset Customers**: *Stay in Control ... In any Situation, 4/e*	2011	195.00
9788130918198	Minor	**Coaching and Counseling**: *Become a Better Manager Through Mentoring, 4/e*	2011	195.00
9788130918273	Decker	**Communication Skills for Leaders**: *Deliver a Clear and Consistent Message, 4/e*	2011	225.00
9788130918143	Kindler	**Conflict Management**: *Resolve Disagreement at Work, 4/e*	2011	165.00
9788130918280	Conlow & Watsabaugh	**Creating a High Performance Team**: *Gain the Skills of Today's Successful Leaders*	2011	225.00
9788130918334	Feldman	**Critical Thinking**: *Make Strategic Decisions With Confidence, 2/e*	2011	225.00
9788130918426	Flynn	**E-Mail Management**: *Keep Your Inbox Under Control, 2/e*	2011	245.00
9788130918471	Kravitz & Schubert	**Emotional Intelligence Works**: *Think, Be and Work Smarter, 3/e*	2011	245.00
9788130918150	Maddux	**Ethics in Business**: *Manage With Authority and Fairness, 2/e*	2011	195.00
9788130918235	Rouillard	**Goals and Goal Setting**: *Achieve Measurable Results, 4/e*	2011	195.00
9788130918204	Conlow Watsabaugh	**Handling Difficult People and Situations**: *Lead People Through Adversity*	2011	195.00

2

ISBN	Author	Title	YOP	Price
9788130918433	Wendover	**High Performance Hiring**: *Select the Best Every Time, 3/e*	2011	245.00
9788130918402	Shea	**Making the Most of Being Mentored**: *Mentors Help Mentees Do, 2/e*	2011	245.00
9788130918242	Scott	**Managing Personal Change**: *Stay Positive and Stay in Control*, 3/e	2011	195.00
9788130918341	Haynes	**Meeting Skills for Leaders**: *Make Meetings More Productive, 4/e*	2011	225.00
9788130918440	Shea	**Mentoring**: *Make It A Mutually Rewarding Experience, 4/e*	2011	245.00
9788130918525	Shandler	**Motivating the Millennial Knowledge Worker**: *Help Today's Workforce Succeed in Today's Economy*	2011	395.00
9788130918167	Mandel	**Presentation Skills**: *Captivate and Educate Your Audience, 4/e*	2011	195.00
9788130918518	Pokras	**Problem Solving for Teams**: *Make Consensus More Achievable, 3/e*	2011	295.00
9788130918259	Haynes	**Project Management**: *Get from the Idea to Implementation Successfully, 4/e*	2011	195.00
9788130918372	Martin	**Quality Customer Service**: *Satisfy Customers– It's Everybody's Job, 5/e*	2011	245.00
9788130918457	Lightle & Doucet	**Sexual Harassment in the Workplace**: *Create a Better Workplace For Everyone, 3/e*	2011	245.00
9788130918501	Lengefeld	**Study Skills Strategies**: *Get the Most From Every Minute of Learning, 4/e*	2011	250.00
9788130918358	Conlow & Watsabaugh	**SuperSTAR Customer Service**: *It's all about C.A.R.E.*	2011	225.00
9788130918297	Maddux & Wingfield	**Team Building**: *Turn Personal Strengths Into Group Success, 5/e*	2011	225.00
9788130918464	Finch	**Telephone Courtesy & Customer Service**: *Be Your Company's Lifeline to Customers, 4/e*	2011	245.00
9788130918389	Conlow & Watsabaugh	**Telephone Skills that Satisfy Customers**: *Unleash the Full Potential of the Telephone*	2011	245.00
9788130918303	Romero	**The Business of Listening**: *Become a More Effective Listener, 4/e*	2011	225.00
9788130918365	Chapman & McKnight	**The New Supervisor**: *Lead With Confidence, 5/e*	2011	225.00
9788130918266	Haynes	**Time Management**: *Get An Extra Day a Week*	2011	195.00
9788130918419	Gill & Chatton	**Understanding Financial Statements**: *Master the Tools That Help You Succeed, 3/e*	2011	245.00